The Perpetual Fear of Ending Up Alone

Written & Illustrated by
Samantha Johnson

For my older sister and built-in best friend Kali,

Thank you for always supporting me through every nook and cranny of my life thus far. I could never repay you for the unwavering encouragement, patience, empathy, and love you have given me. You are the soul person I trusted with this book, even when it was just scribbles in the back of my school planner, and I have never regretted that for a single second. Thank you for coming on this exceedingly long journey with me in creating this art, enduring this pain, and healing these wounds. None of this would have been possible without you. I love you forever.

Part One: Innocence

Wisteria

Climbing the plant
In opposite directions.
Gripping leaf to leaf,
Vine to vine,
A journey of a century.

The seed has flourished
From bloom to blossom,
And petal to floret.
A fragrant wisp,
And an everlasting bliss.

We are Prince,
Bathing in the Purple Rain,
Whipped with immortality.
Guiding each other
Through the flora.

Monarch

I don't know where I'm going
I don't know why I'm here,
But you're around me all the time
To make sure that I get there.
I'm not sure there is a there
As I continue up this hill,
But you assure me that this path is right
Your presence strengthens my will.
As I'm striding solo through sun rays
Hair blowing in the lonesome breeze,
You send the brewing storm away
And put my mind at ease.
My aim is steady and firm
But I fear my target is transparent,
You're there to help me squeeze the trigger
Killing my fear of being errant.
Though my world is corrupted with change
There is one part that remains consistent,
That is your support and unceasing touch
Despite us being strikingly distant.

Lovely

A lovely pair set out on a walk one lovely day,
The lovely pair came across many lovely things along the way.
Through their travels they observed a lovely frog,
A lovely flower,
A lovely home,
A lovely cat,
And many other lovely things.
The most monumental, lovely thing the pair came across,
Was a lovely fork in the road,
Lovely, isn't it?
The lovely man in the lovely pair suggested they split up,
Each of them would travel a different lovely path,
The lovely woman just nodded her head,
And skipped down the path on her left.

A vile pair set out on a walk one vile day,
The vile pair came across many vile things along the way.
Through their travels they observed a vile frog,
A vile weed,
A vile home,
A vile cat,
And many other vile things.
The most monumental, vile thing the pair came across,
Was a vile fork in the road,
Vile, isn't it?
The vile woman in the vile pair forced them to split up,
Each of them must travel a different path in sight,
The vile man didn't get another word in,
And started his way towards the right.

The lovely woman found a lovely, little village on the left path,
Where the weather always seemed to be warm,
Though she sometimes missed her old partner,
There were new relationships here to form.
Every lovely house had lovely flowers outside,
Lovely leaping frogs croaked all throughout the night.
The lovely woman even found a lovely pet kitten,
And, to her vile old life, the woman said, "Good riddance."

The vile man found a vile, smoky city on the right path,
Where the quiet nights were deafening,
Sometimes he was reminded of his old partner,
Whom he would never admit to missing.
Every vile alley was filled with vile, homeless cats,
Vile, slimy frogs under vile weeds they sat.
The vile man dwelt in nothing but a vile shack,
And, to his lovely old life, he said, "I want it back."

Desire

An invisible force,
An undeniable need,
A planted seed.

Love

A four-chambered fuel,
A swarm of butterflies,
A blossomed flower.

Heartbreak

An inexpressible aching,
A broken wine glass,
A wilted plant.

Impossible

I'm going to the beach for the first time ever, but I don't know it yet.
I arrive and stick my toes deep into the pale sand.
I feel its warmth and comfort. It's everything I've ever needed.
A sensation in my gut tells me this is where I'm meant to be, this beach was hand-crafted for me.
The cool wind swipes my quickly sun-kissed skin as I walk further.
My feet are gripped by the sand below with each step I take, yet I'm not struggling to walk at all.
Then, I see the water.
It's deep blue color contrasts with the lighter sky above,
That salty scent it leaves lingering in the air,
Waves crashing, calling my name,
I see no flaws, it's perfect.
I continue my journey towards the sea,
The sand cools the closer I get,
At the edge, it is practically mud.
A wave tip toes up to me and lures me in. There is no way I could have denied the individualized invitation.
Meeting the ocean was a feeling all in itself, but getting to know it was a whole new mannerism.

As I stride deeper, I begin to feel deeper too. I wonder if the sea feels deeply like it's darkest depths or shallowly like it's drying tide pools?
My presence invites an occasional crab, but they don't bother me.
They only pull back the curtains, displaying a new set of perfections the ocean has in store.
I sense a change within me.

Hypnotized, I continue further, not noticing the water is now up to my chin. One large wave could bury me instantly.

This may worry most people, but not me. My connection with the ocean is too strong, it could never hurt me…

Right?

Suddenly, there are fish biting at my legs.

There are gulls swarming, squawking, pecking at my eyes.

There are even more crabs, now crushing my toes with their claws.

There are sharks sinking their sharp teeth into my wet skin.

There I was, drowning in this ocean, being torn apart by its creatures, yet still so in love.

I cannot breathe, but I still gasp for air.

I try pulling myself back onto the beach, but it seems inconceivable.

Eventually I get out.

Eventually I cut ties.

I am horrified, hurt, soaked, sobbing, damaged.

I stand on the beach, on the edge of the ocean, thankful for my survival.

Spectating the sea from its shore, I still see all of its perfections, despite if I don't want to,

Despite what it put me through.

I try closing my eyes, but it's like my eyelids are transparent. I can still sense the deep blue waters in front of me.

I open my eyes and form an idea:

To turn around.

I turn and face the sand dunes and the rest of the land beyond them. I try and pinpoint all of its perfections instead.

The heat,

The cities,

The nature,

The culture.

Any time a thought of the ocean crashes into my head, I drown it out with a thought of the land instead.

I even want to take a few steps towards the land for a moment,

But I don't.

It occurs to me how many negatives the land truly has.

The pollution,

The trash,

The arguments,

The people.

A tap on my shoulder reminds me the sea doesn't have any negatives,

It's perfect.

With slight hesitation, I turn my back to the land and face the sea once more.

Immediately, my clouded head clears,

The waves are calmer,

There are no more sharks,

Or gulls,

Or fish,

Or a single crab in sight.

The tide has gone out, revealing all the shells beneath, making me reminisce even more.

I stick a toe into the white foam.

I know we are both scared,

I know we both know this is right,

I know everyone else would disagree.

I take a few steps back into the forever salty water.

Getting to know the sea was a whole new mannerism, but leaving it behind was impossible.

First Love

After four years, she caught the first spark,
Which soon evolved into a flame.
After four years of yearning to feel the warmth,
To feel the tenderness of the soot on her face,
And the enchantment of the orange glow.
She inhaled the smoke and the youth,
Cherishing every moment, every flare,
Until she got too close.
She felt something hot on her shoulder,
That rapidly spread all over,
Did she relish or despise the sensation?
Her clothes turning to dust,
The aroma of burning hair,
The agony of burning flesh,
Yet her heart remained filled with passion,
As it watched her essence engulfed by flames.
So beautifully brutal,
Magnificently merciless,
And after four years,
Only to be left as a pile of ashes,
With the soul of a phoenix.

"Too Meaningful"

I bought you a rose,

> At the quaint little florist
>
> Oddly placed on Main Street.

I bought you a rose,

> Petals blushing like me
>
> Anticipating our first meet.

I bought you a rose,

> The scent it exuded
>
> I imagine you to.

I bought you a rose,

> Implying you complete me
>
> With that singular bloom.

I bought you a rose,

> To gift to you that day
>
> And with it my heart set free.

I bought you a rose,

       Which I left in solitude

       Just as you did to me.

I bought you a rose,

       Lack of water killing it

       Lack of you is killing me.

I bought you a rose,

       That even in death

       Remained smooth and silky.

I bought you a rose,

       At the time I didn't know

       Would signify so much

I bought you a rose,

       And I'm telling you now

       To ensure my unceasing touch.

(Un)Trustworthy

The effect you have on me is rare,

The control you have over me is astonishing,

How'd you get the girl with trust issues

>   To trust you so easily?

>   So quickly?

>   So much?

You untangle my wires that I tie into knots,

I release for you like the petals of a blooming rose,

How'd you get the girl with trust issues

>   To trust you so intensely?

>   So uniquely?

>   So unimaginably?

I hear you breathe the words I've pined for,

Hoping my past mistakes won't be mirrored,

How'd you get the girl with trust issues

>   To trust you?

Weeping Willow

I'm lost in the forest of your green eyes,
Coaxed in by their hypnotic hue,
But I'm not searching for an exit,
I'm hiking further in.

> The lush vegetation brushes my skin,
> As softly as I imagine you would,
> Like the delicate silkiness of the dew-covered spiderwebs,
> They dangle around me, teasing me like your licked lips.
> My hands grip the nearest tree trunk to regain stability,
> Yet I feel your rough, calloused hand in mine instead.
> Deep in the forest, the vines creep up my calves,
> Wickedly wrapping themselves around my thighs,
> Pulling me into your mossy earth below,
> My body is soaking with mud, but I don't mind.
> Spores float through the air like glitter,
> I breathe them deep into my lungs,
> And breathe out with fungus and ferns.
> My limbs tingle as your insects march through my veins,
> Through my once bloody heart.
> My eyes warp into wildlife watering holes,
> As I sink further and further into you.

Because I'm lost in the forest of your green eyes,
Too far gone now, there's no escape,
Your earth has consumed me from the inside out,
As if I am a mere corroding corpse.

Part Two: Reflection

Bones

Everyday
As you walk the planet
And witness its people,
Whether strangers, peers or friends,
A recurring reality for each
Resides in the back of your brain:
Every individual your eyes touch,
They all have bones.
Can you see their bones?
No.
But that does not mean
They do not
Exist.

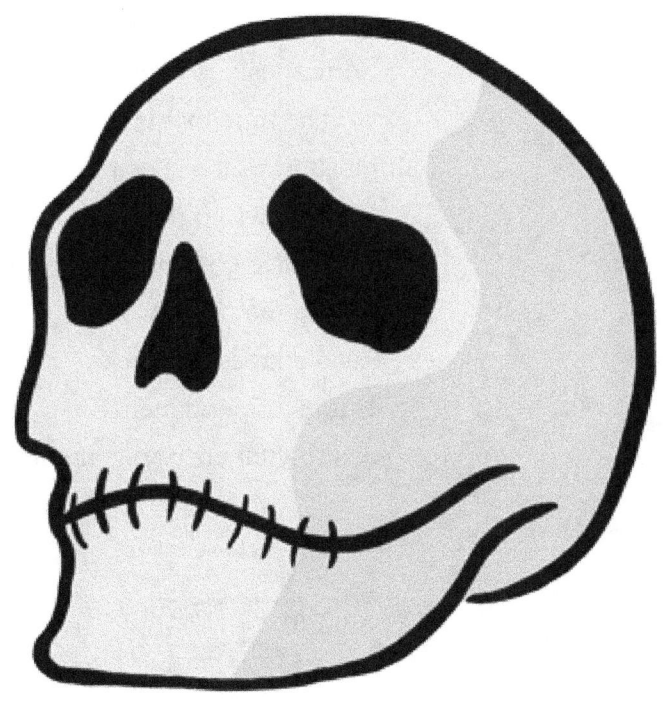

Traffic Jam

The sun rises
Dragging up clouds
Of exhaust with it,
Sounds of engines,
Sirens and horns
Pollute the morning air,
Dew dries up
Streets fill up
Wheels dig up pavement.
An unwavering cycle,
Red, yellow, green,
Which will it be?
Swerving from lane
To lane until
Traffic floods the highway,
Solicitously glaring at
The time that is
Falling short of the speed limit.
Windows go down
Music goes up
Make the most of it,
Road congestion sucks
But its impermanence
Reroutes to vital encouragement.

Marconi

A self-destructive family
In dire need of
A vacation during
A villainous pandemic.

A beach with
Never-ending sand dunes
Limitless crashing waves
Teeming with serotonin seals.

A small, oddball town
With art and its artists
Booming with confidence
Living in tranquility.

An average girl
Reaching for authenticity
Bearing her baggage
Leaving it to drown.

Nostalgic

I am from piles of well-loved stuffed animals,
From bookshelves filled with words too advanced,
From grainy VHS tapes of princess movies,
And too many messy-haired dolls.

I am from a yard full of clover and wildflowers,
From my favorite black wiffleball bat,
From once-white plastic lawn chairs,
And the hammock that became a spider web.

I am from the glance of Bayberry Street through the trees,
From the puddle of a pond down those mossy stairs,
From quick trips to the market for groceries,
And to the ice cream parlor for extra hot fudge.

I am from platefuls of purple potatoes,
From the aroma of garlic in Mom's sauce,
From Dad's tin of cashews by the rusty swing set,
And cake for breakfast on birthdays.

I am from blaring music and even louder singing,
From the open windows blowing our hair,
From ferociously dancing in the backseat,
And driving towards the distant, fiery sunset.

You'd Agree

You're a firework show,
Captivating a rural town.
Your lights shine into eyes,
That reflect the colors back at you.
    Everyone watches in awe,
    Of the way you glimmer and gleam,
    Yet I'm still convinced,
    The reason you do it is only for me.

You're the Super Bowl,
Reeling an entire country.
Some eyes on the ball,
Others wait patiently for halftime.
    Everyone watches in awe,
    Of the way you bring people together,
    Yet I'm still convinced,
    The reason you do it is only for me.

You're the New Year's Ball Drop,
People stay up all hours for you.
You shimmer above your crowd,
Who cheer as you fall towards them.
    Everyone watches in awe,
    Of the way you inflict hope,
    Yet I'm still convinced,
    The reason you do it is only for me.

You're the Moon Landing in '69,
The whole world is eagerly spectating,
As you conquer unclaimed land,
Setting the bar higher than ever imagined.
    Everyone watches in awe,
    Of the way you create the future's history,
    Yet I'm still convinced,
    The reason you do it is only for me.

You're The Beatles on Ed Sullivan,
The fans are psychotically devoted.
Even the biggest haters are tuned in,
To witness this once-in-twenty-lifetimes spectacular.
    Everyone watches in awe,
    Of the way you've captured our world,
    Yet I'm still convinced,
    The reason you do it is only for me.

After so, so long,
I'm so stupidly convinced,
The reason you still do it is for me,

    But I think you might agree.

Selfish

I know you have it worse
I know this hit you hard
I know your heart and trust are broken,
I know this is about you.
I know you don't see eye to eye
I know your tears are flowing
I know I'm not the victim here,
I know this isn't about me.

Yet here I am thinking,
Replaying it in my head
About the feelings I am feeling,
When all you feel is dead.
Am I selfish for thinking of me,
While I'm clearly just a spectator?
I just know you have many ears
While I'm stuck with my thoughts later.
Am I selfish for thinking of me?
Should I be putting you first?
I know I can't be too selfish
If I admit you have it worse.

Therapy Street

If you keep picking at a scab, will it ever heal?
Will it still fix itself if you continue to break the seal?
To win the war but for the enemy I continue to kneel,
To have somehow burnt all my hard-earned barriers of steel,
To mix red and yellow and foolishly expect to create teal,
To have painted the walls and in time watch them peel,
To spend all day cooking yet not get even a taste of the meal,
To say the words aloud makes it seem too real,
And with that I'm not yet sure how to deal.
That's where my mind travels when I discuss how I feel.

I have a roommate who is a little bit weird,
It's as if one day, they sort of just appeared.
I have a roommate who is quite an introvert,
Lounging in bed all day like a tossed t-shirt.
I have a roommate who gets away rent-free,
Only because with them, it's like living with nobody.
I have a roommate who might be jealous of my friends,
They make me feel guilty for staying out late on weekends.
I have a roommate who must be insecure,
They shout comments at me that are very immature.
I have a roommate who can be rather judgmental,
When they shattered my mirror, I don't think it was accidental.
I have a roommate who is fatigued and worn down,
But they've never been to the only gym in our town.
I have a roommate who has the most negative outlook,
When I try to chat with them, they're a tightly sealed book.
I have a roommate who I leave at home all night,
My logic being out of mind if out of sight.
I have a roommate who whenever I return is there,
Still on their bed with that blank yet distressed stare.
I always assumed my strange roommate was rare,
Turns out, they are living rent-free everywhere,
And with everyone, which is completely unfair,
Because the only thing occupying their drawers is despair.
I have a roommate who I'm sending to reside elsewhere,
So, if they knock on your door next, beware!

Little Things

Depression made me stop enjoying things I used to enjoy,
But not things I noticed or expected.
I didn't wake up one day and stop loving Taylor Swift,
Or music in general,
Or art,
Or watching movies,
Or playing board games.
It wasn't obvious to the people around me because I still got out of
bed everyday,
I didn't let myself go or pout in solitude for hours.
It was the little things for me that expired,
Like dancing in the kitchen while my mom makes dinner,
Or singing in the car so loud that my throat is sore the next day,
I stopped laughing in predicaments that would normally leave me in
stitches,
My sister stopped hearing me making up pointless songs while I
showered,
My frantic organization slowly slipped from my mind and my life.
You won't realize you ever stopped doing the little things until you
start doing them again,
Which will make you wonder why you ever stopped.
That's how I know I have healed,
I have improved,
I dance again,
I obnoxiously sing again,
I laugh too hard in stupid situations,
I resumed making up ridiculous songs in the shower,
I rediscovered my state of organization.

The one thing that always made me think I was okay,
Was that I wasn't losing interest in the things I love.
Now I see I was looking at the obvious.
You may not realize you weren't okay until you are,
Because it is always the little things.

The Ocean

Anxiety inducing and reducing
Like the beat of the billows of brine,
The tide creeping in and out
Taking a mouthful of sand with it,
The current giving and taking
Waves with the motion of your lungs.

Gulls swim in the sky,
Fish fly through the sea,
Do they meet at the offing eventually?

Red shoulders scattered in the sand
Green plants colonize below,
Soon enough the sky becomes yellow.
The ocean is a mirror
Wind creeping through the weeds,
The pink clouds follow its lead.
Waves swallow the sun,
Yet the sun tests the water
Before sinking in.
Will it still burn under the sea?
Will it still burn for the ones who need?
One last deep breath,
But do you consume it,
Or does it consume you?

I wrote about it twice…

You bought me a rose,
> But the plans we made
> I couldn't carry out.

You bought me a rose,
> And told me it was
> Too meaningful to write about.

You bought me a rose,
> Which this time you didn't
> Have to dispose of.

You bought me a rose,
> That symbolized the
> Rebloom of our love.

You bought me a rose,
> The scent it exuded
> Was so light and pure.

You bought me a rose,
> Its long-lasting effect
> Is something I can ensure.

You bought me a rose,
> Pinned up by a string
> In my closet for drying.

You bought me a rose,
> The poetic tale and our
> Idyllic love both undying.

Part Three: Solidarity

Closet

My closet
Was once filled with clothes,
All types of clothes,
Mostly shirts and sweaters,
There were bright colors,
Unique designs,
They were my style.
I loved those clothes.

As I grew older,
I grew out of those clothes,
Some became too small,
Some became too childish,
Most of the old clothes were gone,
Very few remained in my closet.

I don't know why,
But I can't seem to refill my closet now.
I've gone shopping in all different stores,
For all different articles,
And there isn't anything my style,
Do I have my own style?
I buy clothes that are decent,
I don't love them,
But they fit well and will make do for now.
I just want clothes that I like,
I want clothes that I love,
I want clothes my style,
In my closet.

Half of Me

We spent seven years
Seven years picking each other apart
Showing each other every inch of our character,
The good, the bad, the ugly, the beautiful,
I had never opened up to someone that much.
I've always had trust issues,
But never with you.
I grew up too early,
With heartbreak, anxiety, depression,
With you by my side.
I've felt betrayal, loneliness, sorrow,
But never like this.

I cut myself in half
Straight down the middle,
Every cut was another secret,
Another joke,
Another promise.
I never hesitated once
I even watched as you mimicked.
We stitched our remaining sides to each other's,
I was me and half you,
You were you and half me,
We were two separate beings,
Yet we were the same person.

Suddenly, I began to feel the stitches loosen, so I attempted to sew us back together only to notice you pulling away and tearing us further apart, I panicked and asked you, "Why? After all this time?" To which you responded with stabs from your scissors and slices at my scarred skin you had, not too long ago, helped me heal and you snipped and pulled and ripped and wriggled at all those intricately interlaced stitches we wove together, until a single one remained. Using the last bit of my strength, I surrendered, waving my needle and thread at you like a white flag.

Then, with a glare from your darkened eyes and a flash of your bloodied scissors,

You snipped the final stitch.

You stole my needle and thread and used them to stitch your two halves back to whole.

You snatched my other side, lit a match, and set it ablaze.

I witnessed you walk away from me

While seated in a pile of my own ashes and tears.

Was there a sign I had missed?

Is what you say about me true?

I felt the world around me get dark and cold,

As if the sun was eternally setting.

I felt our secrets being told,

Our jokes becoming old,

Our promises being broken,

And all that you left with me

Was a head full of memories

And a heart ill at ease.

If we cross each others' path,
You'll notice I've since regrown my other half.
The dust has settled and the war has ended,
This situation did not go as intended.
The chapter is over and I've turned a new page,
This is the dawn of a brand-new age.
I've always said, "If it's meant to be, it will be,"
Yet it's still so difficult letting go of the other half of me.

Abandonment is a tough pill to swallow,
But so is the tormenting haunting that follows.
You go to the mall to seek solace and shop,
When the wraith of your traducer compels you to stop.
You blow out the candles atop your party cake,
The smoke creates illusions of that traitorous snake.
You manage a box of keepsakes and photos,
While the apparition stalks you from the darkest shadows.

Memories conflicting
Thoughts contradicting,
Sometimes forgetting about the war
And going to talk to them like before,
When your heart drops from chest to floor
And loss hits like a slamming door.

It's always the little things too
That make it harrowing for you,
Never reciting in-jokes again,
All traditions come to an abrupt end,
It's quite difficult to just pretend
You're fine with losing your best friend.
Now only a remaining residue,
The most permanent type of tattoo
Written on my skull in blue
Forever reminding me of you.

Growing Pain

Every single breath you take
Blows me further and further away
From something I'm grasping so desperately on to,
My skin is blistering and bloodied
So compromised, my hands are slipping,
Your wind increases the treachery
Like lungs inflate a balloon,
A balloon that grows along with my pain,
It's about to burst
As I burst into tears driving home,
There's a hole in my chest
Like the tunnel my car passes under,
So hollow any noise will echo,
Even the condensation splashing on the road
Like my tears splash onto my lap.

Every shaky breath I take
Takes me further and further away,
Breathing has become a chore
Like oxygen ceases to exist anymore,
It slowly dwindled away over time
Like the wick of a candle with no clear enzyme,
Like a poet who never learned to rhyme,
Like a friendship that was once mine.

You Did This to Me

Don't get me wrong,
It's always great to make someone's day,
To be the reason for the smile on their face,
But not everyone deserves your niceties and politeness.
It's normal to grow rough around the edges,
After persistent betrayal and abandonment,
Who says we need to hide
That side of ourselves from the world?

> Just another excuse to pretend to be who we aren't
> Just for the approval of others.

So, when I ignore your texts or look you up and down,
When I hit you with a snide remark or an eye roll,
Know there is someone from my past
That you can thank for that,
Whether it's your friend, your partner, or yourself,
I'll leave that for you to figure out…

I remember making that decision
Too embarrassed for others to know,
But telling you was obligatory
And was really only the sideshow.

The main event was when I heard
How quickly you shared my secret,
Handing it out like a free sample
When I simply urged you to keep it.

Like anyone in my shoes would
I asked, "Why betray me?"
Instead of just apologizing
You challenged my reality.

You convinced yourself and spectators
That you were falsely accused,
You toyed with my heart and mind while knowing
How severely they had just been bruised.

I had receipts that proved
I knew the actuality of it,
Yet somehow I sat there still
And let myself be cruelly gaslit.

You manipulated them to think I'm the sinner
And I'm sure in that you revel,
But glance in the mirror at your fiery hair
'Cause looking back will be the devil.

After seeing people converse about
If they're the hero or the comic relief,
I've come to realize I'm the lonely villain after a somber self-debrief.
A witty mastermind who chooses the dark side over light,
Fighting protagonists by day and her demons by night.
Everyone who's ever abandoned me, I chased them away,
I'm the delightful host of the apocalyptic doomsday.
I blame others but I ripped myself apart,
These tears for my losses can't thaw my frozen heart.
A criminal vixen who's overuse of the pity card,
Is a sly manipulation used as a safeguard.
The act that I care for you is my signature trap,
The second we disagree, that's when I snap.
I release my flying monkeys and let out a cackle,
You can't get away; you're trapped in my shackles.
With my own bare hands, I rip out your heart,
You wish you knew who I was from the start.
The second your soul exits, I fall to the floor,
Feeling sorry for myself, the root of the war.
I'm always putting on my most terrifyingly brutal mask,
When really, I want a hug but I'm too scared to ask.
Calling myself a villain when I'm a disgraceful deception,
Saying I'm the victim when it's a clear misconception.
But does playing the victim create a villain out of me?
Or do I self-sabotage because I enjoy feeling lonely?

Redshirt

Wondering if karma exists
When my adversaries are living
While my heart is only beating.

My mouth lacks new words and stories,
My eyes have seen no new places or faces,
With no goals and no friends,
With little money and motivation,
Using my time to ruminate on people and predicaments of the past
That no longer carry meaning for anyone but me.

Why am I this way?
Why am I the redshirt in everyone's movie?
And when do I get my spin off?
Why am I the map that leads them to the one?
And when do I unearth my treasure?
Why am I this way?

Part Four: Tragedy

Why I'm Wary

I cannot decipher the greater betrayal:
What she did to me,
Or that you are okay with what she did to me.

Victim

I said we'd meet again
I'm no longer sure that's true,
I'm certain you'd see me but
I would hesitate to see you.

Time went by quicker than light
As I blankly gazed at the clock,
Every half an hour or so
One of us gathered the courage to talk.

Your eyes on me ignited anxiety
As I felt the breakage in your tone,
I reminded myself I wasn't doing this for your closure
I was doing it for my own.

You're not always going to be the victim
My feelings should be valid too,
Like when I told you, "No," countless times
And you heard it as, "Continue."
I struggled, sacrificed, and strained
Yet of course our demise is my fault,
I think it's time you blame yourself
And not me for that assault.
So, if a future someone tells you "No,"
Just as I did repeatedly that day,
Promise me you'll care for them,
Promise me you'll obey.
I may be feeling shattered now
But future me will be okay,
I can't forgive you yet, love
But maybe I will someday.

Your Garage

I tried to hide my vulnerability
But seeing your face dripping with tears,
Of your own and from the sky,
I became jealous and added mine.
Together that night,
We cried once more
We hugged once more
We kissed once more
We felt once more.
All the lights in sight were smudged
And as I reached for my car door,
You walked away.
As you walked away,
You took the warmth with you
The comfort with you
My love with you.
I closed the door,
The car door too,
And I left my pain in your garage,
Then gasped for air as I drove away,
Into the smudged lights.

Just the Payphone

We met on a rainy night,
Though the stars lit your path to me,
The splash of your steps grew louder,
A sigh of relief was following close behind.
You thanked whatever force you believe in,
As your figure was bathed in the yellowish streetlight from above,
Approaching, your presence lifted the dank city humidity.

You were quick to grab me,
It made me nervous,
    But I allowed it.
Change rattled in your pockets as your fingers searched for quarters,
Which clacked rhythmically against my cold metal as you slipped
them inside.
How did you already know my love language?

I winced when you pushed my rusted buttons,
They didn't seem to bother you,
You just wrapped my cord around your warm hand as if your touch
didn't reform me.
So nonchalant,
Which made me nervous,
    But I allowed it.

Then came the same droning noise that always comes,
That ringing, it's born deep inside me,
Some place under all that chipped paint and fingerprints,
Some place I cannot control.
I loathe it,
      But I need it,
I needed it then to whisper to me your true intentions,
It all made sense when the fog lifted
And the light above us flickered,
Because when she picked up on the other end,
When her soft voice hummed you a, "Hello?"
That was all the confirmation I needed.

So, you finished your conversation,
Ended by arguing who loves who more,
Then you left me hanging there,
As you had always planned to.
Alone, I swayed in the rain,
It cinematically fell quicker and quicker
As you walked further and further down the sidewalk,
Your smile growing bigger and brighter,
And with a train of thunder,
With a whistle of lightning,
My streetlight blew out
And a raindrop rolled off my smooth plastic.

Our relationship was anything but consistent,
But the topic of eyes always was.
You informed me that you read somewhere
That your pupils dilate when you look at someone you love.
I only snickered and looked the other way,
Laying on your bed together after our first date.
We practiced eye contact with each other
Because I'm stitched with anxiety,
Eventually I found comfort within ours.
"Your pupils are dilated,"
I remember you saying it
With a sly, gradually growing grin,
You knew I had fallen in love.

All those times you pointed out the dilation of my pupils,
I looked deeply into yours,
Searching for dilation,
Searching for that love in return.
I guess in a way your eyes tried to warn me.
They desperately tried to tell me you were never in love,
Yet your mouth always said differently.
You expressed inconsistently,
While I probably expressed too consistently.
Now that I let you go with pupils still swollen,
Now that you've moved on in two weeks time,
I can see we both need to work on our eye contact skills some more.

Spring

"We have spring memories,
What's so different about summer?"

That vernal chapter haunts me.
After the cold winter came the budding and flowering of our love.
It was thawing with the rest of the flora as you labeled it perennial.
I visualized a peak seedtime primrose,
Struggling through the roughest of winters,
Only to resprout the following spring.
With you, everything felt fresh,
Places I'd been hundreds of times,
Activities I'd done thousands of times,
But this was a springtime feeling.
As the days grew longer, our love shrunk.
The heat from that early summer sun
Caught our primrose in a drought.
I tried to water it, but you plucked it from the earth before I could.
I clung to our memories like dirt clings to freshly pulled roots,
And I was reminded that all beginnings,
No matter how beautiful,
Are always followed by endings.

So, what's so different about summer?
I guess it's just too damn hot.

The Wishing Well

That innocent autumn day
When you took a vulnerable chance
And showed me your safest spot,
A wishing well in the middle of the woods.
I was touched and intrigued
Until you started climbing in,
Then my anxiety grew.
Thousands of questions ran through my mind like water,
Despite that, you took my hand,
And I took your encouragement.
You allowed me to enter first,
A polite mannerism I assumed.
Together, we climbed down the humid well.
At some point during our journey,
You appeared deeper than I,
You asked me to hurry,
For you had already reached the bottom.
We both knew the fastest way for me
To make it to the bottom,
   To you,
     Was to fall.
With very little hesitation, I released my grip,
The wet air brushed against me
   As I hit the water
     With a splash.

After a few gasps of air and a sigh,
I reached out for your hand
Which quickly became a mire vine
On the cold stone walls
Surrounding me.
I squinted towards the small circle of light from above
Which was eclipsed by your silhouette.
"A second chance?" I said stretching towards the sky,
Towards you.
"For me."
You spit the words at me.
I realized there was no escape
From your wishing well.
A single spark of hope still flickered within me,
Maybe you would save me...
Instead, you flicked your last penny into the stone hole,
And as it sharply struck me on the forehead,
  You sashayed away
    Stranding me indefinitely.

It's summer now,
I've began crafting few escape plans,
Most are flawed.
I've caught the attention of few passers-by,
But their pennies only bounced off my compromised skin.
I am now haunted by your words,
Echoing through the damp stone,
The water below, my constant reminder,
The sunlight above, my only hope.

Silver Lake

Laying flat and stagnant
At the bottom of Silver Lake,
I only move to flinch
At the volcanic crack of heartache.

The water begins to boil
Below me the earth tares in two,
Lava pours like blood from veins
The red contrasting with the sky's blue.

I'm finally drowning
While simultaneously burning alive,
Viciously scorched and killed
As the water heals and revives.

The infinite cycle
A purgatory so torturous,
Left longing for land
And a life that is virtuous.

Captive

I agree when they tell me it shouldn't be this hard this young,
But then you tower over me with your persuasive tongue,
It poisons mine through passionate collisions and backhanded praise,
It spits a "Forever," the cancels family holidays.

I agree when they tell me if you wanted to you would,
Yet I witness you criticizing the movie I voiced as good,
You shout your disapproval of my interests from the city rooftop,
I'm grounded in the alleyway below begging you to stop.

I know my relationship shouldn't mirror a heartbreak song,
But I've made unbreakable promises that keep us intact and strong,
Your chains so persistent, I could never rip them apart,
Hence, for now, I will stay a prisoner to your heart.

Caged Verse

This distress is something I have incurred,
Reminiscing on our immutable past,
Set free from one cage,
Only to be imprisoned in the next.
The iron bars of nostalgia and loss,
The cold cement of echoes and tears,
All circulated by the dusty air of broken promises
And invisible goodbyes.
I etch my words into the surrounding stone,
Never reading them aloud,
Because speaking them into existence
Makes it all too real.
I'm unsure how my heart or my mind would react to that.
Thus I will sit in this incurred tomb,
Eyes sinking further in with each tear released,
And I will write myself a path through this misery,
As if I am as free as the verse.

Third time's a charm...

I'm a simple rose,
>   Who grew to become
>   A symbol of love.
I'm a simple rose,
>   A symbol of something
>   They fell short of.
I'm a simple rose,
>   I started off
>   Being left astray.
I'm a simple rose,
>   Who eventually was
>   A part of a bouquet.
I'm a simple rose,
>   And in order to thrive
>   Inside their glass vase.
I'm a simple rose,
>   That was chopped from my roots
>   Because of my grace.
I'm a simple rose,
>   With a fact these lovers
>   Did forget about.
I'm a simple rose,
>   Who can in fact die
>   In the lack of a drought.

I'm a simple rose,
>>Flourished with petals
>>Who's softness still remains.
I'm a simple rose,
>>Braced by a stem
>>Covered in thorns of pain.
I'm a simple rose,
>>Once hung to dry
>>To act as a souvenir.
I'm a simple rose,
>>Now laid in a paper
>>Bag of drear.
I'm a simple rose,
>>Sent on a journey
>>To inevitable death.
I'm a simple rose,
>>A candid of
>>Their love's final breath.

Lucid

I have such vivid dreams
It's truly great at times,
Like when I win awards,
Meet my heroes,
Or can rescue my cat from a tree.
What is not so great is the flip side:
Vivid nightmares,
Like when I have a miscarriage,
Murder my entire family,
Or am the soul survivor of a gruesome plane crash.
What is even more not so great
Is when you are there.
Since my dreams are so realistic,
I act as I would in reality,
And take you back mistakenly.
Since my dreams are so realistic,
We get our differences erased,
And our toxicities erased.
Since my dreams are so realistic,
I expect you to be there when I wake up,
And instead, I suffer through another break up.

More Than a Woman

I'll never forget the day
My mom and I were in the car
When she casually cranked the volume
When the song I resonate with you began.
I'll never forget the feeling
Of closing my eyes and hearing
Not my mom or The Bee Gees singing
But you with your one-handed grip on the wheel.
I'll never forget the grasp
Of your voice as it strangled me,
It pinned down my wandering hand
Who longed to collide with the skip button.
I'll never forget the sound
Of your voice creeping towards the chorus
The hook blurred my vision with tears
And as I blinked them away,
I'll never forget the epiphany
When I could see it was only my mom
When I could hear the beat of the next song
And I knew it was time to move on.

Future Memories

The only thought bouncing around my skull tonight,
Is us together a year ago today.
You finally convinced me to let you read my writing,
At 2 AM in my dimly lit dorm room.
You sat at my desk and silently flipped through my notebook,
  "What's this one about?"
  "This is actually really good,"
I let you read whatever piqued your interest.
Never in my life have I been so vulnerable, so raw,
I might as well have sliced open my own stomach and let you cradle
my insides.
You stumbled across an older poem,
One I often overlook,
One about feeling guilty and selfish for simply feeling.
That's when you held my hand and my gaze,
And you told me I was wrong,
I was not selfish,
My feelings matter just as much as everyone else's.
Your eyes returned to the pages but mine lingered on you,
I knew a future me would be reliving that moment,
As I felt the present becoming the past,
I felt a love so strong gripping the bars of my rib cage,
I felt my eyes swelling with tears from the validation that had just
casually leapt off of your tongue.
I soaked it all in that night in my dimly lit dorm room,
And carved the way you looked into the deepest crevices of my mind.
To give myself a reality check, I softly grazed your arm,
Which quickly turned into a much-needed embrace,
I swear I heard my broken pieces clicking back into place.

An entire year later and that memory still gives me butterflies,
But it is memories like this that twist my brain into remembering you as somebody else,
As somebody who truly loved me in the same cage-rattling way.
Now I know that someone who loves me would never do what you did to me,
Not once,
Definitely not thrice.
Reminding myself of that can be difficult at times,
Especially during the most difficult of times,
Like right now as I weep and I write and I ruminate.
I'm aware I don't know what I want from life,
I never truly have.
I have never known which path to take,
Hell, I have never seen a path for me to take.
The thought of my future debilitates me,
Flags down my fear of the unknown,
My fear of being alone.
Yet I swear for the smallest speck of time,
For the most minuscule moment in my existence,
Not only did I know what I wanted from life,
But I knew what life was all about.
At 2 AM in my dimly lit dorm room,
You didn't just give me a hug,
You gave me a future,
And that future was you.

It's been a year since we last spoke,
When we gave each other's stuff back,
When I didn't want to see you again so I left the
perfumy paper bag on my front porch.
I regret my immaturity,
And sometimes not seeing you then,
But I know if I did your big brown vortexes would
have sinfully sucked me right back in.
There is a lot I wish I could tell you about,
There is a lot I'm glad you've missed,
I can almost feel the grasp I had on your mind loosen
with time while yours is still firmly in place on mine.
Some days I hope you're well,
Hope you're thriving in the city,
Others, I hope you're awake all hours rewinding our
tragedy and picking apart your decisions like me.
All the changes I make,
3 AM I lie awake,
No matter where I start I'll always be led back to that
truly nauseating mistake.
It's not one of mine,
Actually, it's one of yours,
Or two, or three of yours for which I'm confident
you'd still claim innocence to.
All yearning turns to anger,
Yes, even a year later,
Or five, or ten, or forever because now you have
eternally branded yourself as my trespasser.

Dusty

In an old shoe box
You store what you stole,
What I'll never get back.
You don't display it either,
It's not a trophy to you,
It's stashed away in an old shoe box.
You'll forget that it's there
Until you're cleaning your room
Or packing to move.
You find it collecting dust
And shine it on your t-shirt,
Before calling up your elite friends
To show it off,
To brag.

To dangle it from your filthy fingers
Like it isn't delicate, vulnerable glass
That I pray everyday will break within your grasp
Just so you feel a whisper of the pain.
I want you to feel what it feels
To lose a part of yourself
As your blood spills from your palms,
And in that moment of suffering,
I want you to think of me
As I do you in mine.
    But alas,
    You only smirk as you boast,
    Then pack me away
    In an old shoe box
    Until the next time
    You stumble upon it
    Or crave an ego boost.

Hate Me (please)

I wish you hated me,
That you prayed for my demise,
That you've lived brighter days,
Since the one when we cut ties.

> I want you obsessing over me,
> So bad you can't stand the thought of me,
> You'd wonder if it's me driving,
> Every time you see a green Mini.

I hope you burned my clothes,
And any gifts I ever gave you,
You go to watch your favorite show,
But hit play on deja vú.

> I want you to want me dead,
> Want to only see my body lifeless,
> You think I'm crossing the street ahead,
> And rev your engine in distress.

I hope you rip your hair out,
Whenever I cross your dirty mind,
That when you see my pictures,
You wish that you were blind.

I want your blood to boil over,
When you meet someone with my name,
I know you're not for violence,
But it's I you'd dream to maim.

I hope you're reluctantly single,
'Cause I possess each of your lovers,
I haunt your house, a poltergeist,
You'd shake in terror under covers.

I want you to want amnesia,
You'd do anything to forget,
How perfectly romantic is it,
To be someone's biggest regret?

I wish you hated me,
I wish you couldn't heal,
Any thought of me is better,
Than the indifference that you feel.

Reality?

Recalling us is tougher now,
The fog thickened with time.
It's like recollecting a vague dream,
Or waking with tears from a nightmare
In which you cannot remember.

Weighing each memory
On the scales of reality,
     It must have been a different lifetime
     I must have ditched the other timeline.

Because recalling us is difficult,
Like interpreting the whispers of the past.
Like staring into grainy television static
And seeing the image you hope will be cast.

     If none of it feels real anymore,
     How can I be sure that it happened?
The evidence being
I was left with the feeling
Of emptiness.
An eternal internal void.

Recalling the evisceration is an impossible task,
Yet I feel it daily in phantom pains and scars.
Only traces of what was exist
In the form of a poorly written memoir,
And I never learned to read.

It's times like these when I forget,
"We're done,"
And it's over.
Maybe because I wish it wasn't,
Because, right now, I need you more than ever,
Or maybe it's because my brain is preoccupied
With the processing of glass-shattering,
Thriller-screaming,
And alcohol stains.
Banging on my door,
Telling me he's innocent,
Begging me to open it.
The only thing my hand is on,
Not the doorknob,
But my phone.
Whether I was going to call the police
Or you?
I'm still not sure.

It's times like these when I forget,
"We're done,"
And it's over.
And along with that,
I forget how much you reminded me of him.
How I envisioned you'd be the one claiming your drunken innocence
one day,
An innocence you've claimed before,
An innocence as false as my, "I'm okay,"
I uttered at her as she knocked on my door.
I wish you would knock on my door.

It's times like these when I forget,
"We're done,"
And it's over.
And all the words surrounding those,
All the corrupt, cruel words.
Blue paragraphs of white writing just tearing us to pieces.
Even my own words,
Which I now regret unleashing from my tortured mind,
Letting them march down my veins and through my heart,
Guns loaded and ready to aim.
They escape through my fingertips,
Which tonight reek of liquor and dogs,
And liquor-covered dogs.

It's times like these when I forget,
"We're done,"
And it's over.
But when my memories eventually materialize,
It's times like these when I'm reminded how truly alone I am.
Reminded that you were once a safety blanket for me,
Before you bathed yourself in gasoline,
Before you struck that match,
Before you set yourself ablaze,
Just like everyone else has.

Part Five: Peripheral

False Promises

Another false promise,
How can I be honest,
With the one who taught me to lie?

You said you'd never tell,
Including them as well?
Or is that just an excuse to defy?

I'm on the pedestal you built for me,
Nailed plank and stilt for me,
But now you're playing with fire.

When you open your mouth,
Everything goes south,
Because now you're the liar.

You said I'd be famous someday.
When I shared my drawings,
I'd be the next Dalí.
When I hosted magic shows,
I'd be the next Copperfield.
When I earned straight A's,
I'd be the next Einstein.
When I swam until my fingers pruned,
I'd be the next Ariel.
When I put my feelings onto paper,
I'd be the next Dickinson.
When I sang along in the backseat,
I'd be the next Swift.
When I spoke my only line in the school play,
I'd be the next Streep.
When I swung that plastic black bat,
I'd be the next Babe.
When I showcased my early maturity,
I'd be the next Lincoln.
You said I'd be famous someday,
But never said when that someday would be,
Was that just another empty promise?
Or something you actually did foresee?
Was your vision of my future clouded by love?
Because my future is now and it's not looking too good.
Why am I broke and lonely and mentally unstable?
Shouldn't I be moving to Hollywood?

A House

The little thought behind this choice
Could make it seem impulsive,
These walls cannot be ours
When they feel like someone else's.
A temporary permanence,
A relentless holiday,
How am I to live
When my life is so far away?
Ripped from safety too soon,
Torn away from childhood,
The place where I grew up too fast
Yet snatched away before I could.
The creaks in the floor aren't memorized,
Around floats a permanent chill,
I think I left myself back home
Resting on the windowsill.
The closer I grow to my friends,
The further away they get,
But you got what you wanted,
Who cares if I'm upset?
The smell of paint is constant
I've come to loathe it so much,
The more I hear that goddamn drill,
The more I lose my clutch.
I watch the girl in the mirror
As she meets her hair with comb,
Pondering how or if to tell you
That this house is not a home.

Neighborhood Gossip

My neighbor and I,
Since we live close by,
We're always receiving each other's mail.
I've done the most,
I've contacted the post,
But it's useless, they continue to fail.
I get his frills,
All his overdue bills,
While he's getting my praise and well-wishes.
Like he got the meal,
For a really great deal,
And I'm stuck here washing all his dishes.
I've installed locks,
I've labeled my box,
There's really nothing more that can be done.
Just take my keys,
I'm done paying his fees,
The last solution I have is to run.

Family Boycott

"Relationships are a two-way street,"
I say driving down your one-way,
I'm lost and my directions are wrong,
At least that's what you say.

You feel the need to tell me what I am,
When I'm sure I never asked,
"A snob who uses her family for money,"
Yet you refuse to admit I've been outcast.

Encourage my expression then tell me I'm wrong,
Constantly questioning my sanity,
Strutting around with your bottomless bag of excuses,
Nothing can puncture that vanity.

Your go-to is placing the blame onto me,
Aren't you the supposed adult?
Gaslighting, name-calling, especially by my mother's,
Is that supposed to be an insult?

"Family is everything and should be most important,"
What a cheesy motto to live by,
If you never put any sort of effort towards me,
No matter who, you aren't worth my time.

And if that curves your line or sways your norm,
Sorry, but I'm actually not,
I refuse to apologize for putting me first,
And will continue my family boycott.

You've carefully crafted your list of rules,
Before I was even born,
Dipping that entitled pen in your delusional ink,
Scribbling as the paper scorns.

Every member of your sad little cult,
Can bare that honored weapon,
They shift its shape to their advantage,
When their dreaded foe steps in.

They slice and stab at their opponent's skin,
Or squeeze their throats with it,
They chain them down and guillotine,
Until they will submit.

That carefully crafted list of rules,
Written before I was born,
You expect me to simply conform and comply,
Yet I'm the reason it's torn.

Childcare

I have never wanted children.
The only child I long to care for
Is my broken younger self,
Who lingers close behind me,
Looming in my wake,
In the form of my very own shadow.
Stuck like gum to the bottom of my shoe,
Trying so desperately to be left behind,
A feeling so familiar, so safe to her,
But not what she needs.
What she needs is glue to repair the fractures,
Forgiveness and empathy,
Patience and care,
And time for the glue to dry.

Regurgitated Love

"Why didn't you tell me?"
Why didn't you ask?
Why am I the one expected
To complete every simple task?
Why am I neglectful
When you blurred the line?
Why must I dial your number
When you can't even recall mine?
Why do you seem to vanish
Whenever push comes to shove?
Why do you think I want
Any of your regurgitated love?

I have to stop trying

Why are you punishing me?
Did I do something wrong?
I'm sat in a corner
With soap on my tongue,
Why won't you tell me?

I'm screaming at you
At a solid brick wall,
There's rasp in my voice
There's blood in my lungs,
You can't hear me can you?

Your cliff I leap off again
Just to break my own neck,
Look me up in a dictionary
The definition of insanity,
I've tried time and time again.

I can't let it go
I crave it so deep
Like a primal instinct,
Remember when you cared?
Where did the love go?

It's so easy for them
They're not on their knees
With curdling begs and pleads,
They bite at your hand
But you won't reprimand them.

Reflecting for hours
My tears fill your pool,
Spend your summers swimming
Hope you drown in my sorrow
Just as I have for hours.

I consider the past,
Did I speak out of line?
Did I disappoint you?
Should it still matter
If it's home is the past?

I envision a tomorrow
Where I'm pushing fifty
Where you're pushing daisies,
I miss you as I do now,
Will you text me back tomorrow?

They show me your will
My inheritance is regret,
A blank photo album,
A final push away,
"Do with it what you will."

I'll never know what happened
Looming over your grave
Digging up the dirt
Burying my burden,
Maybe that's what happened.

Like it's my moral right
To catch your fake benevolence
To be your punching bag
To be your missile's false target,
That doesn't make it alright.

You're in major debt to me
You ripped yourself away,
A psychopathic field day
Drooling at my decay,
That's how it seems to me.

What could I have done to you
For you to turn on me like this?
You paint my wool a shade of black
Then stab a knife into my back,
The one who screwed this up was you.

Luggage

My bags are filled with all my clothes
Hefty, bloated, and over-packed,
Got my socks, shirts, shoes and pants
Everything's resting on my back.
My bags go everywhere with me
I'm always lugging them behind,
Together they are triple my weight,
Just something to keep in mind…
My bags aren't the only ones I lug
Now yours are with me too,
Not that I have a solid choice
You leave them with me like residue.
My bags were heavy on their own
But I'm strong enough to help myself,
You throw your bags on top of mine
With zero care about my health.
My bags and yours are aging me quick
I've become weary of being warden,
I'm only who you've forced me to be
I beg you, release me from this burden.

Acrobat

I walk a tightrope of dental floss,
My bloodied feet just slip right across.
Bruised and battered from falling far down,
I relive those few seconds when I hit the ground.

Dangling so high up here with no rest,
Like a dead baby bird hanging out of the nest,
His home made of sticks filled with eggshells once walked on,
Where he was always forced to be the bigger person.

Dangling so high up here with no rest,
When letting people down is what I do best.
An untrained professional attempts the impossible act,
Of balancing everyone else's lives on her back.

When you need my support, you no longer ask,
Now I'm just expected to whip out my mask.
I bottle up and save all my tears,
I'm the chair that is more broken than it appears,
Using any remaining strength
I have to keep you upright.
I must seat you at the dinner table
For your five-course meal and your wine.
I must hold you tall
So you can comfortably dine.
You consume your food unbothered,
You boast so loud
It mutes the sound
Of my screaming stomach,
Who is distressed from knowing
It will never cross your mind
To feed an inanimate object.

The Failed Exorcism of the Shapeshifter

I will be whoever you want me to be,
Just open up your hands and I'll give you the key.
I'll shed this skin for you and slip into a better one,
It may be painful in the moment but it's worth it in the long run.
I'll bulldoze my personality to rebuild it for you,
Everything I've bolted down for you I will unscrew.
Watch me retune my heartbeat until it echoes your favorite song,
Watch me relearn how to walk after you told me I'm doing it wrong.
Watch me valiantly rescue you from your fiery forever prison,
Watch as I force Dante to rewrite his Inferno after we have risen.
If you want me to drown myself with no hesitation I would,
Though just because I will do it doesn't mean that I should.
Set me ablaze to rid yourself of any potential evidence,
I'll shrivel in the heat as I burn like a potent stick of incense.
No matter what you inflict something will always remain in me,
No church's exorcist could remove my people pleasing tendencies.

I miss you

The truth is,
I miss you,
And I miss telling everyone how close we are,
Without it feeling like I'm lying.
I wish someone had warned me,
Though the switch flipped so suddenly,
I'm not sure anyone could have had time.
Why did no one tell me not to take it for granted?
If they did, why did I not listen?
Why didn't they tell me more often?
Why didn't they drill it into my growing brain?
The screws in my skull would have stayed indefinitely.

The truth is,
I miss you,
And I'm sorry if this is somehow my own doing.
Maybe I pushed you away,
Maybe I forgot to listen.
Now I regret everything I did or didn't do,
And I apologize if I failed you.
I pray that I didn't become the part of yourself that you hate,
God, I hope that isn't why you left me astray.

The truth is,

I miss you,

And I've spent my entire life dreading this doomsday,

I'm pretty sure you know that.

I've cowered before the inevitable,

Thinking that would simply prevent it,

Like my thoughts are greater than the universe itself.

They may not be,

But you are to me.

The truth is,

I miss you,

And I hate myself for every time I ignored your existence.

It's a part of growing up, I know,

In my immaturity, I saw immortality,

Now I only see lost time.

I feel the resentment still warm on my cheeks,

Not for you anymore but for myself.

You would tell me not to be so hard on myself,

And together we would weep.

The truth is,

I miss you,

And yet this only feels like the beginning.

You have opened a new door,

The one I had triple-locked.

Being happy for you is something I want to do,

But something I cannot do yet,

For I am frozen in time,

Frost biting at any logic I have left.

My heart has crystallized and is numb,

And I can no longer care for anyone,

Not even myself.

The truth is,

I miss you,

And no matter how big of a tantrum I throw,

You will always be the eye of the storm.

If I lock the rest of the world out,

I'll still give you a key.

Or if you find you have wandered through too many doors,

I'll be the compass that leads you home,

Because that's what you are for me.

The truth is,
I miss you,
And I imagine your wedding more than my own,
With beautifully scented bouquets,
A predictable playlist,
And the dress of your dreams.
I would sacrifice anything for your perfect day,
Your joy is priceless to me.
I have always known,
That day, I will have to make the hardest sacrifice of all,
To give up you,
To officially and legally become your number two.
So, when you finally get to say, "I do,"
Know I will be your something blue.

The truth is,

I miss you,

And I've never felt so alone in my entire life.

I'm so proud of how far you've come,

I'm so elated to witness your success,

I'm so envious of how easy you make it look,

But I'm so tired of losing people,

I'm so sick of mourning the living,

I'm so furious that time has passed,

That we have both aged,

Can you believe we're no longer kids?

I'm so scared to believe,

That this is the beginning of the end,

That you have it all figured out without me,

That I've taken you for granted.

I'm so sorry if I haven't told you recently,

That I love you,

That I appreciate you,

That I couldn't have done it without you.

I'm so sorry if I have seemed apathetic or aloof,

That's very irrational,

That's unhealthy coping,

That's me lying to myself,

And to you.

The truth is,

I miss you.

Part Six: Grave

✛

Time Bomb

tick tick tick
The seconds decrease
and time moves forward.
tick tick tick
With each beat
the closer it gets.
tick tick tick
It's not pressure
but time that ensures,
tick tick tick
The repetitive sound
will reach an end.
tick tick tick
The echoed warning
bouncing through your skull,
tick tick tick
Asking yourself,
"How short is a second?"
tick tick tick
The growing anticipation
slicing at your throat.
tick tick tick
Regret and defeat
biting at your ankles.
tick tick tick
A relentless dread
punctures your puny pride.

tick tick tick
Worrying about
What happens when you-

Suffering the Wrath

Yet another too dark evening,
Praying to a God I don't believe in,
Asking, "What did I do?"
"What did I do to receive such punishment?"
I carve "SOS" into my sickly skin,
I tear a piece off my white paper gown and wave it around.
I feel it so immensely it's tattooed on my soul,
    help me help me help me
Do I have to spell it out for you?
Are you blind to my shipwrecked eyes?
Are you deaf to my disconcerting cries?

I should be imprisoned in solitary confinement,
But I'm not,
So, why does it feel like I am?
I'm as invisible as a ghost,
Should we just make it official?
A shivering cold resides deep in my bones,
Born and raised by a lack of attention.
Maybe I acted up or said something out of line,
A sorry attempt to warm up my insides,
Is that what I'm at fault for?
Is that where I messed up?
All for a single spark of a laugh,
I am eternally doomed to suffer the wrath.

Was it worth it?

Do I think of anyone but myself?

I didn't consider the future, why?

Because I'm frightened?

pathetic worthless absentminded loser

Look what I've done,

Look who I have become,

Look at my hands glazed with my own blood.

Can I fix this broken life I have forged?

I'll tell them there's still hope,

Even if I know there isn't.

I'll beg them for a second chance,

Even if I don't deserve it.

"I swear I'll be better,"

"I swear to redeem myself!"

The torture is promised to end,

Only with the rhythm of my heart.

Storm

The sky gets dark,
The leaves turn up,
The breeze becomes aggressive.

Your thoughts get dark,
Your eyes swell up,
You start to feel aggressive.

The first drop drips,
The humidity is thick,
The weather, how expressive.

The first tear drips,
Your throat feels thick,
You're suddenly more expressive.

There's a thunderous clap,
Then a huge lightning flash,
A tree falls into the road.

Your demons all clap,
As your memories flash,
You sit alone in the road.

Mud puddles have formed,
The quiet after the storm,
That's all for this episode.

Red puddles have formed,
The quiet after the storm,
That's all for this episode.

The Living

Death is a funny thing.

I can feel your judgment scratching at the page, do you disagree?

Is it not funny,

To wake up everyday not knowing if it will be your last? Or their last?

Is it not funny,

To be abandoned by the ones you love, just because their time is up?

Is it not funny,

To be able to shorten your time, but not be able to lengthen it?

Is it not funny,

To gather around the lifeless body, flaunting your abundance of days?

Is it not funny,

To burn or bury said body, or let scientists scavenge it for organs?

Is it not funny,

To confide in a stone or a metal vase about what they no longer have:

Life?

Do you disagree about death being a funny thing?

I believe it's quite humorous for everyone,

Except the living.

H

The image in my mind is ruthless
Of her finding him there,
Under a heavy blanket of muteness
With a permanent blank stare.

He was the strongest man I knew,
No word could describe him more,
The cause of a medical breakthrough,
The protagonist of our war.

We loved your burgers, turkey, and sauce,
Your humor and your helping hand,
How on Earth did we come across
Such an incomparable legend?

I'm so pleased you are free of pain
Free of that dreary curtain room,
Thank you for keeping my Grammy sane,
We all love you to the Moon.

lousy

I heard the news through the heartbeat in my ears,
The part of life that everyone fears,
But I breathed deeply in then out,
Because you'd tell me it wasn't worth worrying about.

We started the car and drove straight to you,
Leaving her Jeep on parking garage floor two,
As the elevator rose, my tears fell down,
What an infrequent sight, you making me frown.

I trudged into the room at an irregular pace,
I saw yours and you saw my face,
I said, "Hello," and then grabbed your hand,
I'm still waiting for your dad joke to land.

But you knew I was there by your side,
You felt the rest of them trickle inside,
You heard everyone reconnecting at last,
And knew you were becoming a part of our past.

"From this day on I'll be with you, healthy or ill,"
"Until death do us part," so she rose to fulfill,
As her hand stroked your head, you slipped away,
We all watched you steal your final breath that day.

117

Yet we all still expected you asleep in your chair,
Or in your seat at the table enjoying an éclair,
The dog will forever be waiting for you at the door,
And I don't have someone to play cards with anymore.

However, I'll never lose all the memories we made,
And the sound of your voice could never fade,
Your sense of humor will live on through me,
Like referring to the tastiest foods as "lousy."

Just know I'll be thinking of you always,
Forever wishing I could go back to the old days,
To give you a hug and hear your, "Ha ha!"
I couldn't have asked for a better Papa.

The ringing in your ears that you can't actually hear,
Mountains of shock form beneath your skin,
Tears slide down to extinguish your fire-set cheeks,
As a salty puddle collects on the tip of your chin.

A lump of emotion settles inside your throat,
Your heart strings yanked with such force they snap,
The world has shattered like fragile glass on pavement,
Not even Darwin could learn to adapt.

The loss of someone with great importance to you,
A single word can't replicate the feeling,
Abandonment, betrayal, cessation, desertion,
Will I ever be able to undertake healing?

Dropped in a desolate desert without supplies,
Howling through the torrid air with muted screams,
The taste of blood from sharp sand in your lungs,
Tears can't lull the flames of the sun beams.

Phantom

It's hard to be haunted
Constantly taunted
By something no one else can see.

You swear that it's there
They only ask, "Where?"
Taking it as a hyperbole.

You let down your pride
In search of a guide
    "I feel like I'm truly transparent."

Speaking concise
She shares some advice
    "Some days the ghost is more apparent."

Haunted

Living in a haunted house
An anomaly of its own,
Though the most unsettling part
Is knowing you're never alone.

Traipsing by the lit furnace
Not feeling warmth but chill,
Swearing you left your keys right there
Like always on the windowsill.

The electric bill is always paid
Yet the lights will always flicker,
An attic trip is incomplete
Without hearing a child's snicker.

You tell your guests your stories
You're quite an amusing host,
They laugh and egg you on a bit
But they do not believe in ghosts.

You seem to be at peace for now
But will they break their truce?
Will they remain nonchalant
Innocently hiding your shoes?

Or someday will you set them off?
Will they make your home their own?
They'll dig another six-foot hole
And top it with your gravestone.

You pound your fists on the wooden door
As dirt sifts from cracks inside,
Living in a haunted house
For that is where you died.

Rigor Mortis

My muscles are tense
I loosen them up
Take some deep breaths,
My heart starts to flutter
I grasp my surroundings
An attempt to feel better,
My fingertips tingle
I slam my eyes shut
To force it to dwindle,
Away but my feet
And arms are now numb
Along with my knees,
Freezing yet hot
An invisible brick
Weighs down my gut,
Irrational thoughts
I struggle to think
My brain only rots,
I second guess
Am I alive?
How close is death?
Unable to move
I lie there stunned
In my living tomb.

Part Seven: Resurrection

The Perpetual Fear of Ending Up Alone

I put on my best face and stand center stage,
I ball my fists; they're tense at my sides.
As the sweat drips down my clammy skin,
The curtains are pulled back,
To reveal me.
Nobody expected a one-woman show,
Not even I did.
It's a full house of eyes of blank stares.
The spotlight finds me like a searching bloodhound,
Highlighting my greatest insecurities for the crowd to see,
Like my perpetual fear of ending up alone,
Then grants them like a birthday wish.
I must be in the candles' flames with the heat vibrating off my cheeks,
Blood rushing, bolting through my rigid body,
Determined to display to my audience my crippling embarrassment,
As fast as it possibly can.

...

Trying to keep people in my life
Is like reaching for balloon ribbons
As they drift off into the infinite atmosphere.
They are no longer within my range,
But I continue grasping at their phantoms.
The cotton clouds snicker above
And mock my hopeless attempts,
They contort themselves to humor each other,
Chittering up there with all of their friends,
So far from the ground, so far from being grounded,
Yet I imagine their ignorance to be quite bliss.

...

Brick by brick, stone by stone,
I built this castle all on my own.
Every nail in wood, every swipe of paint you see,
Was hand-placed by little old me.
I chiseled every gargoyle,
I dug the moat with my bare hands,
I even laid the strong foundation
Upon which the castle stands.
Infiltration ceases to exist here,
Yet the people inside have migrated elsewhere.
They do it in the black of night
While I'm wrestling a nightmare.
This morning when I woke,
Everyone was gone.
How could they leave behind
This paradise I built?
How could they leave me here
Without an ounce of guilt?
If this is what they want for me,
Maybe it's what I deserve,
That's when I realized I hadn't built a castle at all,
I had built a prison, and it's time I must serve.
Thus, I chained the gates indefinitely,
I boarded every window,
It didn't matter if I left or not,
There was no place for me to go.
I crept up on my throne of velvet,
That's where I'll eternally sit,
For I have dug my own grave,
And now I must lay in it.

Scarecrow

I stand here in solitude,
A straw man in the corn,
Black birds roost upon my arms,
Always leaving my flesh torn.

The single job I'm given,
Is the one I fail to do,
Forever crucified upon these planks,
For being a mundane statue.

Sinking in my sea of ears,
None of them learned to listen,
My words aren't heard anyways,
Locked up in my mental prison.

With molten sun and near drought,
Have I descended below?
Have I made too many mistakes?
Someone resurrect me if so…

'Cause dry hay catches fire,
And crops must face the harvest,
I stand in a barren aftermath,
But solitude can still infest.

The Engineer

I craft my bridges of fire
So they'll collapse on my command,

Constant signals of smoke
For flagging down my fear.

I always keep my distance
In case of wandering sparks,

They'll burn for millennia
But I'll always return to the dark.

A criminal will find a way in
Even when you've locked the door,
They will find an open window
And creep across the wooden floor,
Their mission is quite simple
To snag your most treasured belongings,
To make your life a living hell,
To never right their wrongdoings,
Keep your bedroom door cracked
They will slip into your dreams,
Watching over while you sleep
Being utterly silent by any means.

But then you're labeled crazy
While checking cameras with cops,
When you see yourself on film
Destroying your home, your jaw drops,
You swear, beg, and cry
As they tighten those cold metal shackles,
Lit with red and blue, you hear
A cryptic voice in your mind cackle.

Insanity

Your smile alone could lock me away in a padded room,
Don't let me out, don't let me free,
My guilty pleasure, my self-inflicted tomb,
I love it here so I swallowed the key.

The lower my chances are, the more I am enthused,
You've got me begging on my hands and knees,
In every love song you are the muse,
Your existence is the most pleasurable tease.

You captivate me like a solar eclipse,
I shouldn't be looking but I truly can't help it,
Just a string coiled around your fingertips,
Please sew me into your favorite outfit.

I'm so envious of the clothes you wear,
They're oblivious of their coveted privilege,
Imagine our fingers wrapped in each other's hair,
Watch your step of all my heart spillage.

This may go a little bit further than obsession,
Can no longer tell if I want you or want to be you,
My inner thoughts advise discretion,
In my most sinful moments I've pictured you.

But honestly I'm a shrew in lion's clothing,
I long for you yet I'd never let you know that,
In my padded room with only my self loathing,
I daydream you're not just someone I gaze longingly at.

Callout

I search my screens for validation,
I build my boundaries on a weak foundation.

I only seek bonds that are parasocial,
I am full of thoughts but never vocal.

I still have no clue what I'm working towards,
I copy my outfits from Pinterest boards.

I earnestly recite every cliché,
I hyper-fixate on something new everyday.

I am my only and own confidant,
I am flakier than a fresh croissant.

I must perfect every new skill I try,
I can no longer control what I do or don't buy.

I own a guitar that only collects dust,
I am a grown adult relearning how to trust.

I start projects just to leave them incomplete,
I have years-old texts in case I need receipts.

I listen to music from the same five artists only,
I isolate myself then complain that I'm lonely.

I tell people details about which they don't care,
I call myself out because at least I'm self aware.

From the Operation Room

Trust issues are something I always thought I had,
And I'm not indefinitely wrong,
But when it comes to offering my heart to another,
Those issues don't seem to prolong.
    I meet someone and sense that connection
    Then instinctively rip out the organ,
    I entrust the crime scene within their grasp
    And accept the unbalanced bargain.
    The surgery begins steady and calm
    But within moments intricacies are unveiled,
    A critically unresponsive condition,
    Even the greatest doctor would've failed.
    They move on to their strategic Plan B
    As they obliterate my offering of love,
    Smashing, crushing, ripping, demolished,
    Now just some rubble to dispose of.
In this time of healing for my heart,
I must learn to entrust my own grasp, then,
Self-love will prepare me for new connections,
And my heart won't lay in malicious hands again.

Found Family

While sulking alone it fell into my lap,
An opportunity like a rain droplet,
Shining bright white in my gentle palm,
I was finally victorious after all the roulette.
Cherished like a sunrise in a bottle,
True proof that astrology is real,
Every star in every sky aligned that night,
An experience truly surreal.
A people not frightened by my monsters,
Instead, they show me theirs too,
Lenient with my limits, have mutual respect,
After all this time, is it really true?
The blood in our veins is contrary,
But our hearts all beat the same rhythm,
You helped me up after that final blow,
Then carried me home to your safe glowing prism.

137

I Shuffled My Deck

I start my evil scheme
By being open-handed,
Unveil my point of view,
Proclaim I'm feeling stranded.
My concern is irrelevant,
My distress is discarded,
I am negativity
I shouldn't have started.
We lash out like lions
Then suddenly silence,
Everything we built
Is gone in a glance.
You left me abandoned
With no one to turn to,
I became despondent,
But if only I knew…
Your knife to my neck,
Your look of despise,
Made me shuffle my deck,
A blessing in disguise.
The leaderboard was foggy,
I didn't know who'd won,
While accepting my trophy,
Out came the sun.
This is a new beginning,
My metamorphosis,
A time for engineering
My new self confidence.

Until the End of Time

I wrap my yarn around polished pins
To knit together my many loose ends,
I weave with calloused fingertips,
Ignoring my hard work unraveling.

I set the table with polished plates
With chalices filled tall with poison,
Freshly squeezed from my infested brain,
I watch as my guests drop like flies.

I dust my display of polished plaques
To remind myself of when I used to win,
I wish to be someone else's trophy,
Instead of just a consolation prize.

I dip the tip of my polished pen
Into the chambers of my beating chest,
I see myself reflected on the page,
As the ink from my shattered heart bleeds.

Personal Renaissance

To dip my brush in paint,
To dip my pen in ink,
   To release the chains I wrapped myself in
   And the words I'm too frightened to think.
To rewind the tape inside my head,
To see not gash but scar,
   To finally watch it through to the end
   And witness the long-awaited title card.
To never pine for a party thrown,
To instead throw one for myself,
   To have endured every moment from cover to cover
   And put the book back onto the shelf.
To thrive at all my peaks,
To unravel in my valleys,
   To eulogize my valiant triumphs
   And create art of all my tragedies.
To befriend my reflection,
To give her what she wants,
   To enter a brand-new era,
   A personal renaissance.

Author's Note

In third grade, my teacher would have us routinely complete an assignment where we would choose a poem from one of her many books, read it aloud to the class, and explain to everyone why we chose that poem. That was my first introduction to poetry, but it wasn't until fourth grade where I was assigned to write my first poem. I remember choosing to write about a baby mouse we had found struggling in our yard. We fed him, cared for him, and nursed him back to health, until one morning we woke up and found him dead. In my fourth-grade class, I wrote about how it was a miracle we found him and he found us, about the love my family had grown to have for him, and about the heartbreak of having my newest friend ripped away so soon. It was tragic for me, and, even at nine years old, I felt this instinct to write about the tragedy. After I poured my growing heart out, I felt better, lighter even. I acknowledged this feeling and put a pin in it, because it wasn't until fifth grade where this cycle became a familiar one to me. The first time I wrote a poem in my free time, not for a school assignment, but for myself, is such a prominent memory. I was having a particularly difficult day and landed on trying to write as a way to cope with it. And it worked, just as it had for the mouse. In fifth grade, writing had solidified itself for me as a means of releasing any pent-up emotion I had, and with that came the idea of one day releasing a book. I knew that year and every year that followed that whatever I was writing would someday lead me to this book. The work in this collection spans from my tenth year of life all the way to my twenty-first. Every emotional moment in that eleven-year chapter was recorded somewhere on a piece of paper, a stray note in my phone, or a typed computer document. I thumbed through those moments and chose the ones I felt were the most raw and passionate, which are what you (hopefully) just read. That being said, if you are someone who is or was a part of my life at any point, and if you feel anything on these pages is about you, I can neither confirm nor deny that fact. But, I can thank you. Whether it was words of love, hate, or indifference that you picked up on, I want to thank you for making me feel something. You are or were pivotal enough to me and to my heart that it translated its beats into words. You are one of the pieces that made up the puzzle that is this book that I am so proud of. Whether I still see you on the daily or I'll never see you again, thank you. Furthermore, thank you for taking the time to read what I had to say, even if you may not agree. One aspect I knew I needed to keep intertwined through this collection was authenticity to myself. I made it a point not to censor myself, to change as little as I possibly could from the original drafts in order to stay true to how I was feeling within those moments. I set out to validate myself through freely expressing how I felt, even if I no longer feel that way. This project was truly a healing journey for me. It was knowing that, through my peaks and my valleys, I had an unwavering way to express my realest self. That someday, I would be willing to share those emotions with the world, and that day has finally come to fruition. My hope is that you are able to find comfort, inspiration, or even yourself within these pages as I did. Thank you for letting me have a slice of your precious time, for helping me open this bottle I've kept sealed for so many years, and for making my dream come true.